CW00430513

Prayers of
St Thomas More

with
A Treatise on the
Holy Eucharist

*All booklets are published thanks to the
generous support of the members of the
Catholic Truth Society*

CATHOLIC TRUTH SOCIETY
PUBLISHERS TO THE HOLY SEE

Contents

What is Owed to Caesar
and what is Owed to God?

*From the address of Pope Benedict XVI to politicians
and civil society, Westminster Hall, 17 September 2010*

Mr Speaker, … As I speak to you in this historic setting, I think of the countless men and women down the centuries who have played their part in the momentous events that have taken place within these walls and have shaped the lives of many generations of Britons, and others besides. In particular, I recall the figure of Saint Thomas More, the great English scholar and statesman, who is admired by believers and non-believers alike for the integrity with which he followed his conscience, even at the cost of displeasing the sovereign whose "good servant" he was, because he chose to serve God first. The dilemma which faced More in those difficult times, the perennial question of the relationship between what is owed to Caesar and what is owed to God, allows me the opportunity to reflect with you briefly on the proper place of religious belief within the political process.

This country's Parliamentary tradition owes much to the national instinct for moderation, to the desire to achieve a genuine balance between the legitimate claims of government and the rights of those subject to it. While decisive steps have been taken at several points in your history to place limits on the exercise of power, the nation's political institutions have been able to evolve with a remarkable degree of stability. In the process, Britain has emerged as a pluralist democracy which places great value on freedom of speech, freedom of political affiliation and respect for the rule of law, with a strong sense of the individual's rights and duties, and of the equality of all citizens before the law. While couched in different language, Catholic social teaching has much in common with this approach, in its overriding concern to safeguard the unique dignity of every human person, created in the image and likeness of God, and in its emphasis on the duty of civil authority to foster the common good.

And yet the fundamental questions at stake in Thomas More's trial continue to present themselves in ever-changing terms as new social conditions emerge. Each generation, as it seeks to advance the common good, must ask anew: what are the requirements that governments may reasonably impose upon citizens, and how far do they extend? By appeal to what authority can moral dilemmas be resolved? These questions take us directly to the ethical foundations of civil discourse. If the moral principles underpinning the democratic process are themselves determined by nothing more solid than social consensus, then the fragility of the process becomes all too evident - herein lies the real challenge for democracy.

…The central question at issue, then, is this: where is the ethical foundation for political choices to be found? The Catholic tradition maintains that the objective norms governing right action are accessible to reason, prescinding from the content of revelation. According to this understanding, the role of religion in political debate is not so much to supply these norms, as if they could not be known by non-believers – still less to propose concrete political solutions, which would lie altogether outside the competence of religion – but rather to help purify and shed light upon the application of reason to the discovery of objective moral principles. This "corrective" role of religion vis-à-vis reason is not always welcomed, though, partly because distorted forms of religion, such as sectarianism and fundamentalism, can be seen to create serious social problems themselves. And in their turn, these distortions of religion arise when insufficient attention is given to the purifying and structuring role of reason within religion. It is a two-way process. Without the corrective supplied by religion, though, reason too can fall prey to distortions, as when it is manipulated by ideology, or applied in a partial way that fails to take full account of the dignity of the human person. Such misuse of reason, after all, was what gave rise to the slave trade in the first place and to many other social evils, not least the totalitarian ideologies of the twentieth century. This is why I would suggest that the world of reason and the world of faith – the world of secular rationality and the world of religious belief – need one another and should not be afraid to enter into a profound and ongoing dialogue, for the good of our civilization.

Religion, in other words, is not a problem for legislators to solve, but a vital contributor to the national conversation. In this light, I cannot but voice my concern at the increasing marginalization of religion, particularly of Christianity, that is taking place in some quarters, even in nations which place a great emphasis on tolerance. There are those who would advocate that the voice of religion be silenced, or at least relegated to the purely private sphere. There are those who argue that the public celebration of festivals such as Christmas should be discouraged, in the questionable belief that it might somehow offend those of other religions or none. And there are those who argue – paradoxically with the intention of eliminating discrimination – that Christians in public roles should be required at times to act against their conscience. These are worrying signs of a failure to appreciate not only the rights of believers to freedom of conscience and freedom of religion, but also the legitimate role of religion in the public square. I would invite all of you, therefore, within your respective spheres of influence, to seek ways of promoting and encouraging dialogue between faith and reason at every level of national life.

Your readiness to do so is already implied in the unprecedented invitation extended to me today. And it finds expression in the fields of concern in which your Government has been engaged with the Holy See. In the area of peace, there have been exchanges regarding the elaboration of an international arms trade treaty; regarding human rights, the Holy See and the United Kingdom have welcomed the spread of democracy, especially in the last sixty-five years; in the field of development, there has been collaboration on debt relief, fair trade and financing for development, particularly through the International Finance Facility, the International Immunization Bond, and the Advanced Market Commitment. The Holy See also looks forward to exploring with the United Kingdom new ways to promote environmental responsibility, to the benefit of all.

The Death of St Thomas More

by William Roper (1626)[*]

So remained Sir Thomas More in the Tower, more than a seven-night after his judgment. From whence, the day before he suffered, he sent his shirt of hair, not willing to have it seen, to my wife, his dearly beloved daughter, and a letter written with a coal (contained in the foresaid book of his works), plainly expressing the fervent desire he had to suffer on the morrow, in these words following: 'I cumber you, good Margaret, much, but would be sorry if it should be any longer than tomorrow. For tomorrow is St Thomas even, and the Utas of St Peter, and therefore tomorrow I long to go to God: it were a day very meet and convenient for me. Dear Megg, I never liked your manner better towards me than when you kissed me last. For I like when daughterly love and dear charity hath no leisure to look to worldly courtesy.'

And so upon the next morrow, being Tuesday, St Thomas his eve, and the Utas of St Peter, in the year of our Lord 1535, according as he in his letter the day before had wished, early in the morning came to him Sir Thomas Pope, his singular good friend, on message from the king and his council, that he should before nine of the clock of

Sir Thomas More, by Hans Holbein

the same morning suffer death; and that, therefore, he should forthwith prepare himself thereto. 'Master Pope,' quoth Sir Thomas More, 'for your good tidings I heartily thank you. I have been always much bounden to the king's highness for the benefits and honours that he had still from time to time most bountifully heaped upon me; and yet more bounden am I to his grace for putting me into this place, where I have had convenient time and space to have remembrance of my end. And so help me God, most of all, Master Pope, am I bounden to his highness that it pleaseth him so shortly to rid me out of the miseries of this wretched world, and therefore will I not fail earnestly to pray for his grace, both here, and also in the world to come.' 'The king's pleasure is farther,' quoth Master Pope, 'that at your execution you shall not use many words.' 'Master Pope,' quoth he, 'you do well to give me warning of his grace's pleasure, for otherwise, at that time, had I purposed somewhat to have spoken; but of no matter wherewith his grace, or any other, should have had cause to be offended. Nevertheless, whatsoever I intended, I am ready obediently to conform myself to his grace's commandment; and I beseech you, good Master Pope, to be a mean to his highness, that my daughter Margaret may be at my burial.' 'The king is content already,' quoth Master Pope, 'that your wife, children and other friends shall have liberty to be present thereat.' 'Oh, how much beholden then,' said Sir Thomas More, 'am I unto his grace, that unto my poor burial vouchsafeth to have so gracious consideration!' Wherewithal Master Pope, taking his leave of him … could not refrain from weeping. Which Sir Thomas More perceiving, comforted him in this wise: 'Quiet yourself, good Master Pope, and be not discomforted, for I trust that we shall once in heaven see each other full merrily, where we shall be sure to live and love together, in joyful bliss eternally.'

Upon whose departure, Sir Thomas More, as one that had been invited to some solemn feast, changed himself into his best apparel. Which Master Lieutenant espying, advised him to put it off, saying, that he that should have it was but a javill.[1] 'What, Master Lieutenant?' quoth he, 'shall I account him a javill that will do me this day so singular a benefit? Nay, I assure you, were it cloth of gold, I should think it well bestowed on him, as St Cyprian did, who gave his executioner thirty pieces of gold.' And albeit, at length, through Master Lieutenant's importunate persuasion, he altered his apparel, yet, after the example of the holy Martyr St Cyprian, did he, of that little money that was left him send an angel of gold to his executioner.

And so was he by Master Lieutenant brought out of the Tower, and from thence led towards the place of execution. Where, going up the scaffold, which was so weak that it was ready to fall, he said merrily to the

Lieutenant: 'I pray you, Master Lieutenant, see me safe up, and for my coming down let me shift for myself.' Then desired he all the people thereabout to pray for him, and to bear witness with him, that he should now there suffer death in and for the faith of the holy Catholic Church. Which done, he kneeled down, and, after his prayers said, turned to the executioner with a cheerful countenance, and said unto him: 'Pluck up thy spirits, man, and be not afraid to do thine office: my neck is very short, take heed, therefore, thou strike not awry, for saving of thine honesty.' So passed Sir Thomas More out of this world to God, upon the very same day which he most desired.

Soon after his death came intelligence thereof to the Emperor Charles. Whereupon he sent for Sir Thomas Eliott, our English ambassador, and said to him: 'My Lord ambassador, we understand that the king your master hath put his faithful servant, and grave wise councillor, Sir Thomas More, to death.' Whereupon Sir Thomas Eliott answered that 'he understood nothing thereof.' 'Well,' said the Emperor, 'it is too true: and this will we say, that had we been master of such a servant, of whose doings ourselves have had these many years no small experience, we would rather have lost the best city of our dominions, than have lost such a worthy councillor.' Which matter was, by the same Sir Thomas

Eliott to myself, to my wife, to Master Clement and his wife, to Master John Heywood and his wife, and unto divers others his friends accordingly reported.

A Godly Meditation

*Written by St Thomas More while he was a prisoner
in the Tower of London, 1534*

Give me thy grace, good Lord.
To set the world at nought,
To set my mind fast upon thee.
And not to hang upon the blast of mens' mouths.
To be content to be solitary,
Not to long for worldly company,
Little and little utterly to cast off the world,
And rid my mind of all the business thereof.
Not to long to hear of any worldly things,
But that the hearing of worldly fantasies
may be to me displeasant.
Gladly to be thinking of God,
Piteously to call for his help,
To lean unto the comfort of God,
Busily to labour to love him.
To know mine own vility and wretchedness,
To humble and meeken myself
under the mighty hand of God,
To bewail my sins passed,
For the purging of them, patiently to suffer adversity.
Gladly to bear my purgatory here,

To be joyful of tribulations,
To walk the narrow way that leadeth to life.
To bear the cross with Christ,
To have the last thing in remembrance,
To have ever afore mine eye my death
that is ever at hand,
To make death no stranger to me,
To foresee and consider the everlasting fire of hell,
To pray for pardon before the judge come.
To have continually in mind the passion
that Christ suffered for me,
For his benefits uncessantly to give him thanks.
To buy the time again that I before have lost.
To abstain from vain confabulations,
To eschew light foolish mirth and gladness,
Recreations not necessary to cut off.
Of worldly substance, friends, liberty, life and all,
to set the loss at right nought,
for the winning of Christ.
To think my most enemies my best friends,
For the brethren of Joseph could never have done
him so much good
with their love and favour as they did him
with their malice and hatred.
These minds are more to be desired of every
man than all the treasure of all the princes and kings,
Christian and heathen, were it gathered
and laid together all upon one heap.

A Devout Prayer

*Written between his condemnation
on 1st July 1535 and his execution five days later.*

Pater Noster. Ave Maria. Credo.

OHoly Trinity, the Father, the Son, and the Holy Ghost, three equal and co-eternal Persons, and one Almighty God, have mercy on me, vile, abject, abominable, sinful wretch: meekly knowledging before thine High Majesty my long-continued sinful life, even from my very childhood hitherto.

In my childhood, in this point and that point, etc. After my childhood, in this point and that point, and so forth by every age, etc.

Now, good gracious Lord, as thou givest me thy grace to knowledge them, so give me thy grace, not in only word but in heart also with very sorrowful contrition to repent them and utterly to forsake them. And forgive me those sins also, in which by mine own default, through evil affections and evil custom, my reason is with sensuality so blinded that I cannot discern them for sin. And illumine, good Lord, mine heart, and give me thy grace to know them, and forgive me my sins negligently forgotten, and bring them to my mind with grace to be purely confessed of them.

Glorious God, give me from henceforth thy grace, with little respect unto the world, so to set and fix firmly mine heart upon thee, that I may say with thy blessed apostle St Paul: *The world is crucified to me and I to the world.*[2] *For to me to live is Christ, and to die is gain. My desire is to depart and be with Christ.*[3]

Give me thy grace to amend my life, and to have an eye to mine end without grudge of death which to them that die in thee, good Lord, is the gate of a wealthy life.

Almighty God, *Teach me to do thy will. Make me run after thee in the fragrance of thy anointing oils. Take my right hand and guide me in the straight path because of my enemies. Draw me after thee with bit and bridle; bind fast my jaws when I come not near to thee.*[4]

O glorious God, all sinful fear, all sinful sorrow and pensiveness, all sinful hope, all sinful mirth, and gladness take from me. And on the other side concerning such fear, such sorrow, such heaviness, such comfort, consolation and gladness as shall be profitable for my soul: *Deal with thy servant according to thy steadfast love, O Lord.*[5]

Good Lord, give me the grace, in all my fear and agony, to have recourse to that great fear and wonderful agony that thou, my sweet Saviour, hadst at the Mount of Olivet before thy most bitter passion, and in the meditation thereof, to conceive ghostly comfort and consolation profitable for my soul.

Almighty God, take from me all vain-glorious minds, all appetites of mine own praise, all envy, covetise,[6] gluttony, sloth, and lechery, all wrathful affections, all appetite of revenging, all desire or delight of other folks' harm, all pleasure in provoking any person to wrath and anger, all delight of exprobation or insultation against any person in their affliction and calamity.

And give me, good Lord, a humble, lowly, quiet, peaceable, patient, charitable, kind, tender, and pitiful mind, with all my works, and all my words, and all my thoughts, to have a taste of thy holy, blessed Spirit.

Give me, good Lord, a full faith, a firm hope, and a fervent charity, a love to the good Lord incomparable above the love to myself; and that I love nothing to thy displeasure, but everything in an order to thee.

Give me, good Lord, a longing to be with thee, not for the avoiding of the calamities of this wretched world, nor so much for the avoiding of the pains of purgatory, nor of the pains of hell neither, nor so much for the attaining of the joys of heaven, in respect of mine own commodity, as even for a very love to thee.

And bear me, good Lord, thy love and favour, which thing my love to thee-ward (were it never so great) could not but of thy great goodness deserve.

And pardon me, good Lord, that I am so bold to ask so high petitions, being so vile a sinful wretch, and so unworthy to attain the lowest. But yet, good Lord, such they be, as I am bounden to wish and should be nearer the effectual desire of them, if my manifold sins were not the let.[7] From which, O glorious Trinity, vouchsafe of thy goodness to wash me, with that blessed blood that issued out of thy tender body, O sweet Saviour Christ, in the divers torments of thy most bitter passion.

Take from me, good Lord, this lukewarm fashion, or rather key-cold manner of meditation, and this dullness in praying unto thee. And give me warmth, delight and quickness in thinking upon thee. And give me thy grace to long for thine holy sacraments, and specially to rejoice in the presence of thy very blessed body, Sweet Saviour Christ, in the holy sacrament of the altar, and duly to thank thee for thy gracious visitation therewith, and at that high memorial, with tender compassion, to remember and consider thy most bitter passion.

Make us all, good Lord, virtually participant[8] of that holy sacrament this day, and every day make us all lively members, sweet Saviour Christ, of thine holy mystical body, thy Catholic Church.

Keep us today, Lord, from all sin. Have mercy on us, Lord, have mercy. Lord, show us your love and mercy; for we put our trust in you.

In you, Lord, is our hope: and we shall never hope in vain.[9] Pray for us, O holy mother of God. That we may be made worthy of the promises of Christ.

For my friends

Almighty God, have mercy on N. and N. *(with special meditation and consideration of every friend, as godly affection and occasion requireth)*.

For my enemies

Almighty God, have mercy on N. and N., and on all that bear me evil will, and would me harm, and their faults and mine together, by such easy, tender, merciful means, as thine infinite wisdom best can devise, vouchsafe to amend and redress, and make us saved souls in heaven together where we may ever live and love together with thee and thy blessed saints, O glorious Trinity, for the bitter passion of our sweet Saviour Christ. Amen.

Lord, give me patience in tribulation and grace in everything to conform my will to thine: that I may truly say: *Thy will be done, on earth as it is in heaven*. The things, good Lord, that I pray for, give me thy grace to labour for. Amen.

Prayers from the Treatise on the Passion

The fall of the angels

O Glorious blessed Trinity, whose justice hath damned unto perpetual pain many proud rebellious angels, whom thy goodness had created to be partners of thine eternal glory, for thy tender mercy plant in mine heart such meekness that I so may by thy grace follow the motion of my good angel, and so resist the proud suggestions of those spiteful spirits that fell, as I may, through the merits of thy bitter passion, be partner of thy bliss with those holy spirits that stood and now, confirmed by thy grace, in glory shall stand for ever.

The fall of man

Almighty God, that of thine infinite goodness didst create our first parents in the state of innocence, with present wealth and hope of heaven to come, till through the devil's train[10] their folly fell by sin to wretchedness, for thy tender pity of that passion that was paid for their and our redemption, assist me so with thy gracious help, that unto the subtle suggestions of the serpent I never so incline the ears of mine heart but that my reason may resist them and master my sensuality and refrain me from them.

The decree of man's redemption

O Holy blessed Saviour Jesus Christ, which willingly didst determine to die for man's sake, mollify mine hard heart and supple it so by grace, that through tender compassion of thy bitter passion I may be partner of thine holy redemption.

Introduction to the narrative of the passion

Good Lord, give us thy grace not to read or hear this gospel of thy bitter passion with our eyes and our ears in manner of a pastime, but that it may with compassion so sink into our hearts that it may stretch to the everlasting profit of our souls.

The paschal supper

Good Lord, which upon the sacrifice of the paschal lamb didst so clearly destroy the first begotten children of the Egyptians, that Pharao was thereby forced to let the children of Israel depart out of his bondage, I beseech thee give me the grace in such faithful wise to receive the very sweet paschal lamb, the very blessed body of our sweet Saviour thy son, that, the first suggestions of sin by thy power killed in my heart, I may safe depart out of the danger of the most cruel Pharao the devil.

Christ foretells his passion

Good Lord, give me the grace so to spend my life, that when the day of my death shall come, though I feel pain in my body, I may feel comfort in soul; and with faithful hope of thy mercy, in due love towards thee and charity towards the world, I may, through thy grace, part hence into thy glory.

The priests and ancients conspire against Christ

Gracious God, give me thy grace so to consider the punishment of that false great council that gathered together against thee, that I be never, to thy displeasure, partner nor give mine assent to follow the sinful device of any wicked counsel.

The treason of Judas

O my sweet Saviour Christ, whom thine own wicked disciple, entangled with the devil through vile wretched covetise[11] betrayed, inspire, I beseech thee, the marvel of thy majesty with the love of thy goodness, so deep into mine heart, that in respect of the least point of thy pleasure, my mind may set always this whole wretched world at nought.

'He loved them unto the end'

O my sweet Saviour Christ, which (in) thine undeserved love towards mankind, so kindly wouldst suffer the painful death of the cross, suffer not me to be cold nor luke-warm in love again towards thee.

The disciples find a room for the last supper

Almighty Jesus Christ, which wouldst for our example observe the law that thou camest to change, and being maker of the whole earth wouldst have yet no dwelling-house therein, give us thy grace so to keep thine holy law, and so to reckon ourselves for no dwellers but for pilgrims upon earth, that we may long and make haste, walking with faith in the way of virtuous works, to come to the glorious country wherein thou hast bought us inheritance for ever with thine own precious blood.

The washing of the feet

Almighty Jesus, my sweet Saviour Christ, which wouldst vouchsafe thine own almighty hands to wash the feet of thy twelve apostles, not only of the good but of the very traitor too, vouchsafe, good Lord, of thine excellent goodness, in such wise to wash the foul feet of mine affections, that I never have such pride enter into mine heart as to disdain either in friend or foe, with meekness and charity for the love of thee, to file[12] mine hands with washing of their feet.

Institution of the Holy Eucharist

Our most dear Saviour Christ, which after the finishing of the old paschal sacrifice hast instituted the new sacrament of thine own blessed body and blood for a memorial of thy bitter passion, give us such true faith therein and such fervent devotion thereto, that our soul may take fruitful ghostly food thereby.

A Treatise on the Holy Eucharist

*Written by St Thomas More in the Tower of London in
1534. He entitled it: To receive the blessed body of our
Lord sacramentally and virtually both.*

They receive the blessed body of our Lord both
sacramentally and virtually, which in due manner and
worthily receive the blessed sacrament. When I say
worthily, I mean not that any man is so good, or can be so
good, that his goodness could make him, of very right
and reason, worthy to receive into his vile earthly body
that holy blessed glorious flesh and blood of Almighty
God himself, with his celestial soul therein and with the
majesty of his eternal godhead; but that he may prepare
himself, working with the grace of God, to stand in such a
state as the incomparable goodness of God will, of his
liberal bounty, vouchsafe to take and accept for worthy to
receive his own inestimable precious body into the body
of so simple a servant.

Such is the wonderful bounty of Almighty God that he
not only doth vouchsafe, but also doth delight, to be with
men, if they prepare to receive him with honest and clean
souls, whereof he saith: *Deliciae meae esse cum filiis*

hominum. My delight and pleasures are to be with the sons of men.[13]

And how can we doubt that God delighteth to be with the sons of men, when the Son of God and very Almighty God himself liked not only to become the son of man, that is to wit, the son of Adam the first man, but over that in his innocent manhood to suffer his painful passion for the redemption and restitution of man.

In remembrance and memorial whereof, he disdaineth not to take for worthy such men as wilfully make not themselves unworthy to receive the self-same blessed body into their bodies, to the inestimable wealth of their souls. And yet of his high sovereign patience he refuseth not to enter bodily into the vile bodies of those whose filthy minds refuse to receive him graciously into their souls. But then do such folk receive him only sacramentally and not virtually. That is to wit, they receive his very blessed body into theirs under the sacramental sign, but they receive not the thing of the sacrament, that is, to wit, the virtue and the effect thereof, that is to say, the grace by which they should be lively members incorporate in Christ's holy mystical body, but instead of that live grace they receive their judgement and their damnation.

And some such, by the outrageous enormity of their deadly sinful purpose, in which they presume to receive that blessed body, deserve to have the devil (through the sufferance of God) personally so to enter into their hearts that they never have the grace after to call him out. But like as a man with bridle and spur rideth and ruleth a horse and maketh him go which way he list to guide him, so doth the devil by his inward suggestions govern and guide the man, and bridle him from all good and spur him into all evil, till he finally drive him to all mischief. As he did the false traitor Judas, that sinfully received that holy body, whom the devil did therefore first carry out about the traitorous death of the self-same blessed body of his most loving master, which he so late so sinfully received, and within a few hours after unto the desperate destruction of himself.

And therefore have we great cause with great dread and reverence to consider well the state of our own soul, when we shall go to the board of God, and as near as we can (with the help of his special grace diligently prayed for before) purge and cleanse our souls by confession, contrition and penance, with full purpose of forsaking from henceforth the proud desires of the devil, the greedy covetise[14] of wretched worldly wealth, and the foul affection of the filthy flesh, and be in full mind to persevere and continue the ways of God and holy cleanness of spirit: lest that if we presume so unreverently to receive this precious margarite, this pure pearl, the blessed body of our Saviour himself contained in the sacramental sign of bread, that like a sort of swine, rooting in the dirt and wallowing in the mire, we tread it under the filthy feet of our foul affections while we set more by them than by it, intending to walk and wallow in the puddle of foul filthy sin, therewith the legion of devils may get leave of Christ so to enter into us, as they got leave of him to enter into the hogs of Genesareth; and as they ran forth with them, and never stinted till they drowned them in the sea, so run on with us (but if God of his great mercy refrain them and give us the grace to repent), else not fail to drown us in the deep sea of everlasting sorrow.

Of this great outrageous peril the blessed apostle St Paul giveth us gracious warning, where he saith in his first epistle to the Corinthians: *Quicunque manducaverit panem et biberit calicem Domini indigne, reus erit corporis et sanguinis Domini*: Whosoever eat the body and drink the cup of our Lord unworthily, he shall be guilty of the body and blood of our Lord.[15]

Here is, good Christian readers, a dreadful and terrible sentence, that God here, by the mouth of his holy apostle, giveth against all them that unworthily receive this most blessed sacrament, that their part shall be with Pilate and the Jews, and with that false traitor Judas since God reputeth the unworthy receiving and eating of his blessed body for a like heinous offence against his majesty as he accounted theirs that wrongfully and cruelly killed him.

And therefore to the intent that we may avoid well this importable[16] danger, and in such wise receive the body and blood of our Lord as God may of his goodness accept us for worthy, and therefore not only enter with his blessed flesh and blood sacramentally and bodily into our bodies, but also with his Holy Spirit graciously and effectually into our souls, St Paul, in the place afore remembered, saith: *Probet seipsum homo, et sic de pane illo edat, et de calice bibat*: Let a man prove himself, and so eat of that bread and drink of that cup. But then in what wise shall we prove ourselves? We may not go rashly to God's board, but by a convenient time taken before. We must, as I began to say, consider well and examine surely what state our soul standeth in.

In which thing it will be not only right hard, but also peradventure impossible, by any possible diligence of ourselves, to attain unto the very full undoubted surety thereof, without special revelation of God. For, as the scripture saith: *Nemo vivens scit, utrum odio vel amore dignus sit*: No man living knoweth whether he be worthy the favour or hatred of God.[17] And in another place: *Etiamsi simplex fuero, hoc ipsum ignorabit anima mea*:

If I be simple, that is to say, without sin, that shall not my mind surely know.[18]

But God yet in this point is of his high goodness content if we do the diligence that we can, to see that we be not in the purpose of any deadly sin. For though it may be that for all our diligence God (whose eye pierceth much more deeper into the bottom of our heart, than our own doth) may see therein some such sin as we can not see there ourselves, for which St Paul saith: *Nullius mihi conscius sum, sed non in hoc justificatus sum*: In mine own conscience I know nothing, but yet am I not thereby justified,[19] yet our true diligence done in the search, God of his high bounty so far forth accepteth, that he imputeth not any such secret lurking sin, unto our charge for an unworthy receiving of this blessed sacrament, but rather the strength and virtue thereof purgeth and cleanseth that sin. In this proving and examination of ourself, which St Paul speaketh of, one very special point must be to prove and examine ourself and see that we be in the right faith and belief concerning the holy blessed sacrament itself. That is to wit, that we verily believe that it is, as in deed it is, under the form and likeness of bread, the very blessed body, flesh, and blood of our holy Saviour Christ himself, the very self same body, and the very self same blood, that died and was shed upon the cross for our sin, and the third day gloriously did arise again to life and, with the souls of holy saints fetched out of hell ascended and stied[20] up wonderfully into heave and there sitteth on the right hand of the father and shall visibly descend in great glory to judge the quick and the dead, and reward all men after their works.

We must, I say, see that we firmly believe that this blessed sacrament is not a bare sign or a figure or a token of that holy body of Christ but that it is, in perpetual remembrance of his bitter passion that he suffered for us the self same precious body of Christ that suffered it by his own almighty power and unspeakable goodness consecrated and given to us.

And this point of belief is, in the receiving of this blessed sacrament, of such necessity and such weight, with them that have years and discretion, that without it they receive it plainly to their damnation. And that point believed very full and fastly must needs be a great occasion to move any man in all other points to receive it well. For note well the words of St Paul therein: *Qui manducat de hoc pane et bibit de calice indigne, judicium sibi manducat et bibit, non dijudicans corpus domini*: He that eateth of this bread and drinketh of this cup unworthily, eateth and drinketh judgment upon himself in that he discerneth not the body of our Lord.[21]

L o! Here this blessed apostle well declareth that he which in any wise unworthily receiveth this most excellent sacrament receiveth it unto his own damnation, in that he well declareth by his evil demeanour towards it, in his unworthy receiving of it, that he discerneth it not, nor judgeth it, nor taketh it for the very body of our Lord, as in deed it is.

And verily it is hard but that this point, deeply rooted in our breast, should set all our heart in a fervour of devotion, towards the worthy receiving of that blessed body. For surely there can be no doubt on the other side, but that if any man believe that it is Christ's very body, and yet is not inflamed to receive him devoutly thereby, that man were likely to receive this blessed sacrament very coldly and far from all devotion, if he believed that it were not his body, but only a bare token of him instead of his body.

But now having the full faith of this point fastly grounded in our heart, that the thing which we receive is the very blessed body of Christ, I trust there shall not greatly need any great information farther to teach us, or any great exhortation farther to stir and excite us, with all humble manner and reverent behaviour to receive him.

For if we will but consider, if there were a great worldly prince which for special favour that he bare us would come visit us in our own house, what a business we would then make and what a work it would be for us, to see that our house were trimmed up in every point to the best of our possible power, and everything so provided and ordered, that he should by his honourable receiving perceive what affection we bear him, and in what high estimation we have him; we should soon by the comparing of that worldly prince and this heavenly prince together (between which twain is far less comparison than is between a man and a mouse) inform and teach ourself with how lowly mind, how tender loving heart, how reverent humble manner we should endeavour ourself to receive this glorious heavenly king, the king of all kings, almighty God himself, that so lovingly doth vouchsafe to enter, not only into our house (to which the noble man Centurio acknowledged himself unworthy) but his precious body into our vile wretched carcase, and his holy spirit into our poor simple soul.

What diligence can here suffice us? What solicitude can we think here enough against the coming of this almighty king, coming for so special gracious favour, not to put us to cost, not to spend of ours, but to enrich us of his, and that after so manifold deadly displeasures done him so unkindly by us, against so many of his incomparable benefits before done unto us. How would we now labour and foresee that the house of our soul (which God were coming to rest in) should neither have any poisoned spider or cobweb of deadly sin hanging in the roof, nor so much as a straw or a feather of any light lewd thought that we might spy in the floor, but we would sweep it away.

But forasmuch, good Christian reader, as we neither can attain this great point of faith nor any other virtue but by the special grace of God, of whose high goodness every good thing cometh (for as St James saith: *Omne datum optimum et omne donum perfectum desursum est, descendens a patre luminum*: Every good gift and every perfect gift is from above, descending from the father of lights[22]) let us therefore pray for his gracious help in the attaining of his faith, and for his help in the cleaning of our soul against his coming, that he may make us worthy to receive him worthily. And ever let us of our own part fear our unworthiness, and on his part trust boldly upon his goodness, if we forslow[23] not to work with him for our own part. For if we willingly upon the trust and comfort of his goodness leave our own endeavour undone, then is our hope no hope, but a very foul presumption.

Then when we come unto his holy board, into the presence of his blessed body, let us consider his high glorious majesty, which his high goodness there hideth from us, and the proper form of his holy flesh covereth under the form of bread, both to keep us from abashment such as we could not peradventure abide, if we (such as we yet be) should see and receive him in his own form such as he is, and also for the increase of the merit of our faith in the obedient belief of that thing at his commandment, whereof our eyes and our reason seem to show us the contrary.

And yet forasmuch as although we believe it, yet is there, in many of us that believe, very faint and far from the point of such vigour and strength as would God it had, let us say unto him with the father that had the dumb son: *Credo, domine, adjuva incredulitatem meam*: I believe, Lord, but help thou my lack of belief:[24] and with his blessed apostles: *Domine, adauge nobis fidem*: Lord, increase faith in us.[25] Let us also with the poor publican, in knowledge of our own unworthiness, say with all meekness of heart: *Deus propitius esto mihi peccatori*: Lord God, be merciful to me, sinner that I am.[26] And with the Centurio: *Domine, non sum dignus ut intres sub tectum meum*: Lord, I am not worthy that thou shouldst come into my house.[27]

And yet with all this remembrance of our own unworthiness and therefore the great reverence, fear and dread for our own part, let us not forget on the other side to consider his inestimable goodness, which disdaineth not, for all our unworthiness, to come unto us and to be received of us.

But likewise as at the sight or receiving of this excellent memorial of his death (for in the remembrance thereof doth he thus consecrate and give his own blessed flesh and blood unto us) we must with tender compassion, remember and call to mind the bitter pains of his most painful passion. And yet therewithal rejoice and be glad in the consideration of his incomparable kindness, which in his so suffering for us, to our inestimable benefit he showed and declared towards us. So must we be both sore afeard of our own unworthiness, and yet therewith be right glad and in great hope at the consideration of his unmeasurable goodness.

St Elizabeth, at the visitation and salutation of our blessed Lady, having by revelation the sure inward knowledge that our Lady was conceived with our Lord, albeit that she was herself such as else for the diversity between their ages she well might and would have thought it but convenient and meetly that her young cousin should come visit her, yet now because she was mother to our Lord, she was sore amarvelled of her visitation and though herself far unworthy thereto; and therefore said unto her: *Unde hoc, ut veniat mater Domini mei ad me?* Whereof is this, that the mother of our Lord should come to me[28] But yet for all the abashment of her own unworthiness she conceived thoroughly such a glad blessed comfort, that her holy child St John the Baptist leapt in her womb for joy: Whereof she said: *Ut facta est vox salutationis tuae in auribus meis, exultavit gaudio infans in utero meo*: As soon as the voice of thy salutation was in mine ears, the infant in my womb leapt for joy.

Now like as St Elizabeth by the spirit of God had those holy affections, both of reverent considering her own unworthiness in the visitation of the mother of God, and yet for all that so great inward gladness therewith, let us at this great high visitation, in which not the mother of God, as came to St Elizabeth, but one incomparably more excelling the mother of God than the mother of God passed St Elizabeth, doth so vouchsafe to come and visit each of us with his most blessed presence, that he cometh not into our house but into our self, let us, I say, call for the help of the same holy spirit that then inspired her, and pray him at this high and holy visitation so to inspire us, that we may both be abashed with the reverent dread of our own unworthiness, and yet therewith conceive a joyful consolation and comfort in the consideration of God's inestimable goodness. And that each of us, like as we may well say with great reverent dread and admiration: *Unde hoc, ut veniat Dominus meus ad me?* Whereof is this, that my Lord should come unto me? (and not only unto me but also into me), so we may with glad heart truly say at the sight of his blessed presence: *Exultavit gaudio infans in utero meo*: The child in my womb, that is to wit, the soul in my body, that should be then such a child in innocence, as was that innocent infant St John leapeth, good Lord, for joy.

Now when we have received our Lord and have him in our body, let us not then let him alone, and get us forth about other things and look no more unto him (for little good could he, that so would serve any guest) but let all our business be about him. Let us by devout prayer talk to him, by devout meditation talk with him. Let us say with the prophet: *Audiam quid loquatur in me Dominus*: I will hear what our Lord will speak within me.[29]

For surely if we set aside all other things and attend unto him, he will not fail with good inspirations to speak such things to us within us as shall serve to the great spiritual comfort and profit of our soul. And therefore let us with Martha provide that all our outward business may be pertaining to him, in making cheer to him and to his company for his sake; that is to wit, to poor folk of which he taketh everyone, not only for his disciple, but also as for himself. For himself saith: *Quamdiu fecistis uni de his fratribus meis minimis, mihi fecistis*: That that you have done to one of the least of these my brethren, you have done it to myself.[30]

And let us with Mary also sit in devout meditation and harken well what our Saviour, being now our guest, will inwardly say unto us. Now have we a special time of prayer, while he that hath made us, he that hath bought us, he whom we have offended, he that shall judge us, he that shall either damn us or save us, is of his great goodness become our guest and is personally present within us, and that for no other purpose but to be sued unto for pardon and so thereby to save us.

Let us not lose this time therefore, suffer not this occasion to slip, which we can little tell whether ever we shall get it again or never. Let us endeavour ourself to keep him still, and let us say with his two disciples that were going to the castle of Emmaus: *Mane nobiscum, Domine*: Tarry with us, good Lord:[31] and then shall we be sure that he will not go from us, but if we unkindly put him from us. Let us not pray like the people of Genesareth, which prayed him to depart out of their quarters, because they lost their hogs by him, when instead of the hogs he saved the man, out of whom he cast the legion of devils that after destroyed the hogs. Let not us likewise rather put God from us by unlawful love of worldly winning, or foul filthy lust, rather than for the profit of our soul to forbear it. For sure may we be that when we wax such, God will not tarry with us, but we put him unkindly from us.

Nor let us not do as did the people of Jerusalem, which on Palm Sunday received Christ royally and full devoutly with procession, and on the Friday after put him to a shameful passion. On the Sunday cried: *Benedictus qui venit in nomine Domini*: Blessed be he that cometh in the name of our Lord:[32] and on the Friday cried out: *Non hunc sed Barabbam*: We will not have him but Barabbas.[33] On the Sunday cried: *Hosanna in excelsis*; on the Friday: *Tolle, tolle, crucifige eum*.[34] Sure if we receive him never so well, nor never so 'devoutly at Easter, yet whensoever we fall after to such wretched sinful living, as casteth our Lord in such wise out of our souls, as his grace tarrieth not with us, we show ourself to have received him in such manner as those Jews did. For we do as much as in us is, to crucify Christ again: *Iterum* (saith St Paul) *crucifigentes filium Dei*.[35]

Let us, good Christian readers, receive him in such wise as did the good publican Zaccheus, which when he longed to see Christ, and because he was but low of stature, did climb up into a tree. Our Lord seeing his devotion called unto him and said: Zaccheus, come off and come down, for this day must I dwell with thee. And he made haste and came down, and very gladly received him into his house. But not only received him with a joy of a light and soon sliding affection, but that it might well appear that he received him with a sure earnest virtuous mind, he proved it by his virtuous works. For he forthwith was contented to make recompense to all men that he had wronged, and that in a large manner, for every penny a groat; and yet offered to give out also forthwith the one half of all his substance unto the poor men, and that forthwith also, by and by, without any longer delay. And therefore, he said not: Thou shalt hear that I shall give it: but he said: *Ecce dimidium bonorum meorum do pauperibus*: Lo, look, good Lord, the one half of my goods I do give unto poor men.[36]

With such alacrity, with such quickness of spirit, with such gladness, and such spiritual rejoicing, as this man received our Lord into his house, our Lord give us the grace to receive his blessed body and blood, his holy soul, and his Almighty Godhead, both into our bodies and into our souls, that the fruit of our good works may bear witness unto our conscience that we receive him worthily and in such a full faith, and such a stable purpose of good living, as we be bounden to do. And then shall God give a gracious sentence and say upon our soul, as he said upon Zaccheus: *Hodie salus facta est huic domui*: This day is health and salvation come unto this house: which that holy blessed person of Christ, which we verily in the blessed sacrament receive, through the merit of his bitter passion (whereof he hath ordained his only blessed body, in that blessed sacrament, to be the memorial) vouchsafe, good Christian readers, to grant unto us all.

End notes

- From *The Mirror of Virtue in Worldly Greatness of the Life of Sir Thomas More*

1 worthless fellow

2 *Gal* 6:14.

3 *Phil* 1:21, 23.

4 A series of Old Testament texts including Ps 143:10, Song 1:3 and *Ps* 31:9. In St Thomas More's original these texts are in Latin.

5 *Ps* 118:124.

6 covetousness.

7 hindrance.

8 sharers in the virtue.

9 from the *Te Deum* (Latin in the original).

10 deceit.

11 covetousness.

12 defile.

13 Prov. viii, 31.

14 covetousness.

15 11 :27. The text is quoted incorrectly; the first *and* should be *or*.

16 grave.

17 *Eccles* 9:1.

18 *Job* 9:2l.

19 *Cor* 4:4.

20 soared.

21 1 *Cor* 11:29.

22 *Jas* 1:17.

23 neglect.

24 *Mk* 9:23.

25 *Lk* 17:5.

26 *Lk* 18:13.

27 *Mt* 8:8.

28 *Lk* 1:43.

29 *Ps* 134:9.

30 *Mt* 25:40.

31 *Lk* 24:29.

32 *Mt* 21:9.

33 *Jn* 18:40.

34 *Jn* 19:15.

35 *Heb* 6:6.

36 *Lk* 19:8.

Thomas More

CTS Saints of the Isles

Lord Chancellor of England, Christian Humanist, author of Utopia and loving husband and father; Thomas More's enduring appeal is renewed in this new introductory biography. A talented scholar, lawyer and politician, More rose to the highest position in England under Henry VIII. However, when he was called upon to choose between God and earthly power he remained firm in his faith and was executed as "the King's good servant and God's first". Thomas More was canonised in 1935 and proclaimed patron of statesmen and politicians by John Paul II in 2000.

The Saints of the Isles series brings together telling accounts of the extraordinary lives of men and women from the British Isles - lives of holiness, courage and true discipleship to Christ and the Gospel message.

ISBN: 1 86082 217 7

B 677